Falcons

Text and Photographs by Wayne Lynch
Illustrations by Sherry Neidigh

NORTHWORD PRESS
Minnetonka, Minnesota

IN ALL THE WORLD, there are 61 kinds, or species (SPEE-sees), of falcons. Only five of them breed in the United States and Canada, but they include two of the most famous of these birds. One is the Arctic-nesting gyrfalcon (JEER-fal-con), the largest, most powerful falcon in the world. The other is the crow-size peregrine (PER-uh-gren) falcon, possibly the fastest-flying bird on Earth. The peregrine is also one of the most widespread birds in the world and lives on every continent except Antarctica.

The other three falcons include the merlin, which nests in the northern prairies and forests of Canada and Alaska. The second is the prairie falcon, which lives on the hot, dry western prairies and deserts. The third is the American kestrel (KESS-trel).

The kestrel is the smallest falcon in Canada and the United States. It is only slightly larger than a robin. The kestrel hunts in open areas throughout the two countries as well as in city parks and fields, cemeteries, airports, and golf courses.

Peregrine falcon chicks less than one year old have dark streaks on their feathers. Some of the streaks fade as they get older.

Gyrfalcons often hunt along the edge of the ocean in Canada, as far as 800 miles (1,288 kilometers) north of the Arctic Circle.

Adult American kestrels catch and kill deer mice for a meal.
They may hunt in the grassy ditch beside a highway.

Falcons, like hawks and eagles, are birds of prey (PRAY), or raptors (RAP-ters). They hunt and eat other animals. All five of the falcons in the United States and Canada hunt birds. Some of them specialize more than others.

The gyrfalcon of the Arctic, for example, mainly hunts birds such as willow ptarmigan (TAR-mih-gun) and rock ptarmigan. A family of gyrfalcons may eat 200 ptarmigan during the four months of their summer nesting season. This is the time that young falcons are in the nest and must be fed by their parents.

The merlin, on the other hand, is a fierce hunter of small to medium songbirds such as robins, starlings, swallows, and sparrows. Out West, the prairie falcon hunts horned larks, meadow larks, and mourning doves.

Because the kestrel is so small, it hunts grasshoppers, dragonflies, scorpions, spiders, and lizards more often than it hunts birds. Scientists in New York State, however, watched one kestrel hunting at a colony of nesting bank swallows. It caught chicks as they crowded at the opening of the family nest burrows.

The hungriest swallow chicks would sit as close as possible to the mouth of the burrow so they could get as much food as possible when their parents came to feed them. The kestrel hung upside down above the burrows by one foot and grabbed the chubby chicks with its other foot. In one day, the falcon caught nine swallow chicks in a row while hunting like this. For some of the chicks, it was not a good idea to be so greedy!

The most famous bird hunter among the five falcons is the peregrine. Although this bold raptor commonly hunts shorebirds and ducks, nothing with feathers is safe from attack. Scientists who study birds are called ornithologists (or-nih-THOL-uh-jists). They have made a list of the birds that peregrines eat. In North America, the list includes over 425 species, more than half of the birds that live there. Worldwide, the peregrine hunts more than 2,000 different birds!

The list is even longer if you include those birds that the peregrine doesn't plan to eat and just wants to scare away from its nest and young. If a peregrine parent thinks its chicks are in danger, it will bravely attack birds much bigger than itself, including hawks, owls, ravens, vultures, cranes, and geese. One bold peregrine even attacked a bald eagle, killing it with a blow to its head.

Falcons
FUNFACT:

Hunting falcons commonly miss more prey than they catch. When peregrines hunt fast-flying shorebirds they may only succeed at 1 in 10 attempts. They do better when they are hunting insects and small mammals, which do not see as well as birds.

In the autumn, young and inexperienced ducks are easy prey for peregrine falcons.

Even though the falcons of Canada and the United States prefer birds, they also eat many other creatures. For example, in some areas of the Arctic, gyrfalcons hunt Arctic hares, and peregrines hunt lemmings. On the west coast of Canada, hungry peregrines will even eat green, slimy banana slugs, and kestrels will consume earthworms. Along the Snake River in Idaho, prairie falcons catch so many Townsend's ground squirrels that many prairie falcons are able to nest close together in record numbers.

Falcons are also not afraid of bats. They eat any they can catch, as well as mice, voles, or shrews that scamper into view.

The bare skin at the base of a falcon's beak is called the cere (SER). The yellow cere on this kestrel indicates that the bird is healthy.

Sometimes falcons catch more food than they can eat. When they do, they store the extra meals in a hiding place. This storing behavior is called caching (CASH-ing). Some favorite places for falcons to cache are in crevices on high cliffs, under a bush, in a large clump of grass, in an old raven or hawk nest, or in a hollow tree.

Falcons usually cache extra food any time they can, but they do it most often in the winter and during the summer nesting season when they are busy raising chicks. In winter, high winds and snowstorms make hunting difficult and falcons may not hunt or eat for several days. This is when the food they stored earlier may save their lives.

During the nesting season, parent falcons must catch much more prey than usual because they must feed their hungry chicks many times every day. If the parents have a bad day of hunting they can give the extra food they cached to their chicks. One peregrine that nested in Boise, Idaho, cached more than 20 mourning doves on a building's window ledge near its nest.

Falcons
FUNFACT:

Most falcons have a dark streak on their face below their eyes. This may reduce glare and help the birds see better in bright sunshine. Football players smear black shoe polish under their eyes for the same reason.

Falconers cover the eyes of their birds with a special leather hood when they take them to a new location. This keeps the birds quiet and relaxed.

Perhaps as long ago as 4,000 years, humans began to trap, tame, and train peregrines and other falcons to hunt for them. This was the beginning of the sport we now call falconry. In ancient times, falconry was the sport of kings and emperors. One powerful emperor in ancient China owned 200 gyrfalcons, as well as 300 other falcons and hawks. He had 10,000 workers whose only job was to find prey for his falcons on hunting expeditions.

In those days, falcons were extremely valuable, sometimes worth more than gold. Royalty and other powerful people often used falcons as expensive gifts and rewards. Sometimes falcons were used as payment for ransoms. One captured prince in medieval Europe was freed from prison only after his family delivered a dozen priceless white gyrfalcons from distant Greenland.

Even today, the gift of a rare falcon may impress a king. The royal family of Saudi Arabia has a great love of falconry. In the 1980s, the Prime Minister of Canada gave a white gyrfalcon to the King of Saudi Arabia as a gift of friendship.

Gyrfalcons vary in color from all white with some scattered dark markings on their back to dark gray all over. White birds are most common in the Arctic.

13

Hungry juvenile merlins scream loudly at a parent as it approaches with fresh food in its talons.

Worldwide, the sport of falconry has probably never been more popular than it is today. In the United States and Canada, there are approximately 3,600 falconers. Today most falconers use their birds for sport hunting, but some use them for business. Airports in many large cities, including Chicago, New York, Milwaukee, Montreal, and Vancouver, hire falconers to fly their trained birds over the runways. The falcons scare away gulls, ducks, and geese that can fly into the planes and cause serious accidents or damage.

Falcons hunt in several different ways. The most common way is to sit and wait quietly on an elevated place such as the top of a telephone pole, tree, or cliff. At other times they soar high over their hunting area to search for prey.

All falcons are strong flyers and sometimes they hunt by flying close to the ground using low hills, rocky ridges, and bushes to hide their approach. They hunt like this to surprise birds and animals and scare them into the open where they can be attacked more easily.

Another way for some falcons to hunt is to hover (HUH-ver), but hovering is hard work. The large peregrine is too heavy to hunt this way, but the small kestrel can hover better than any other raptor.

When a flying kestrel locates a meal it may immediately begin to hover, no higher than the roof on a house. A kestrel can hover for as long as a minute, and even longer if there is a strong wind. When the moment is right, the bird drops like a rock and grabs its prey.

An adult peregrine falcon has a wingspan of about 40 inches (1 meter). Male and female peregrines look similar except that the female is larger and heavier.

For many falcon lovers the power dive is the most exciting type of hunting to watch, and peregrines do it best. To see how fast a peregrine could dive, a skydiver who was also a falconer jumped out of a plane with his trained peregrine at 12,000 feet (3,658 meters). That's over 2 miles (3.5 kilometers) high in the sky. As the skydiver did a free fall, the peregrine flew along with him and the man was able to estimate the falcon's speed. With its wings pulled tight against its body, the falcon flew at 200 miles (322 kilometers) per hour. It looked like a feathered rocket! The skydiver was unable to see if the peregrine could fly faster because he had to stop the experiment and open his parachute.

Falcons
FUNFACT:

Many peregrines migrate as far south as Central and South America. They make round trips of over 10,000 miles (16,000 kilometers).

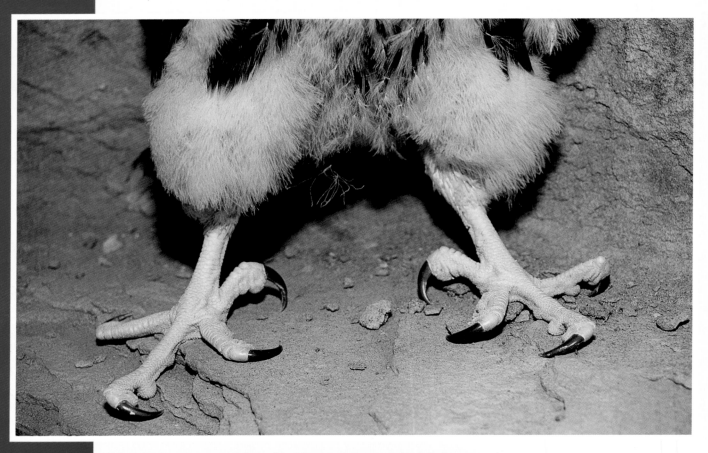

The feet of a one-month-old prairie falcon are almost as large as its parents' feet. But the young bird is still not strong enough to kill for itself.

When a falcon catches its prey, the prey is usually still alive. Like most birds of prey, a falcon has feet that are tough and strong. On the end of each toe is a long, sharp claw, called a talon. Falcons do not kill prey with their feet, but with their sharp beak. They bite the prey on the head or on the back of the neck while holding it in their talons. Hawks and eagles use their long talons and powerful grip to squeeze their prey over and over again until it dies.

All falcons have a special tooth, called a tomial (TOE-mee-ul) tooth, on the sharp edge of the upper beak. Ornithologists believe that falcons use this tooth to cut or injure the spinal cord of their prey when they bite it on the neck. The tomial tooth may help falcons kill prey that is larger than themselves.

Falcons need clean, healthy feathers to hunt and fly fast, and to stay warm in winter and dry in summer. They may spend several hours every day caring for their feathers.

All falcons bathe when they can. A peregrine will step into the water up to its belly at the edge of a stream and dip its head underwater over and over again. At the same time, it raises its feathers, flutters its wings and tail, and lets the water wash over its back. Merlins and gyrfalcons do the same.

Falcons
FUNFACT:

The prairie falcon is usually found far away from water sources. The peregrine falcon is almost always found near a river or lake.

When everything freezes in winter, a gyrfalcon may bathe in soft, fluffy snow to clean its feathers. In the desert where water is scarce, the prairie falcon bathes on the bare ground and dusts its feathers with powdery dirt. Scientists think the dry dirt works like mosquito repellent to keep lice and ticks away. Other falcon species also take dust baths. Researchers watched a merlin that had many lice on its body dust itself seven times in one hour. The lice and ticks feed on the falcon's blood and make the bird itch.

Falcons
FUNFACT:

In captivity, kestrels and merlins may live for 10 years. Prairie falcons, peregrines, and gyrfalcons may live for 20 years or more. In the wild life is much harder and most wild falcons live only half as long as they do in captivity.

The merlin can survive the cold of a northern winter as long as it can find enough food to eat and keep its body warm.

When a peregrine falcon captures prey, it may spread its wings and huddle over the animal. This helps hide it and guard it from other falcons.

Besides dusting their feathers and washing them with water or snow, falcons also wipe a special oil on their feathers. This is called preening. The oil comes from the preen gland, on the bird's rump at the base of its tail.

The falcon gently squeezes the gland with its beak and rubs its head over it. Then it uses its beak and its head to spread the oil to the other feathers on its body. The oil keeps the feathers from drying and cracking, and also protects them from harmful bacteria and fungi that may damage them.

Sleek, shiny feathers are a good clue that a falcon is well fed and healthy. Female falcons need a strong, healthy partner to help them raise their chicks. So, at the start of every breeding season, the females observe males to see which ones would make good partners, or mates.

Some falcons stay with the same partner for many years, and some choose a new partner every year. If a falcon's partner dies or disappears, the remaining bird usually finds another mate quickly.

Peregrines begin to preen when they are just eight days old. As adults they may spend several hours each day caring for their feathers in this way.

American kestrels can hover in one spot for almost one minute. When the wind is blowing strongly they can do it even longer, but it takes lots of energy.

To be a good partner, a male falcon needs more than sleek, shiny feathers. He must also be a strong flyer and a good hunter.

For these reasons, when a male falcon is courting a female he tries to impress her with his flying and hunting skills. He circles and soars high above her, screaming loudly. He performs steep power dives and climbs, and flies past the female as fast as he can, doing difficult half-rolls, dips, and swerves to show off.

This kind of flying takes a lot of strength and energy and if the male is not healthy the female will probably notice.

Sometimes the female joins the male and soars and screams with him. He may climb above her and dive at her over and over again, or chase close behind her in a high-speed race. One peregrine may fly upside down beneath the other and the pair may grab each other's talons briefly. The birds may even touch each other's beak in midair.

Falcons
FUNFACT:

Falcons are quiet most of the year. They use their loud voices mainly during the spring and summer when they are courting, and to frighten away enemies.

A peregrine nest is nothing more than a depression in the sand created by the mother's body. The parents add no sticks, grass, feathers, or greenery to their nest.

When the courting falcons finally land they usually perch, or sit, close together. They may stay like this for hours. Sometimes they preen each other's head feathers, or gently nibble on each other's beak and toes. Once the female chooses a male to be her partner, she sits and waits, while he hunts, and hunts, and hunts.

The male does all the hunting for both of them for at least two months. He may hunt for one whole month before the female lays her first egg, and then continue for another month while she incubates (INK-you-bates) the eggs. After that, he feeds the newly hatched chicks as well as their mother, who needs to stay with the babies to keep them warm.

By the time the baby falcons are about two weeks old their fluffy, down feathers are thick enough to keep them warm. Then the mother can leave and go hunting for herself.

A female falcon sometimes turns upside down to catch the prey dropped by her mate. They both continue flying!

When the male makes a food delivery to his mate it can be spectacular to watch. He may fly past her carrying prey and screaming loudly. If she stays perched where she is, she may scream back at him to bring the food.

Female falcons are always larger and more powerful than their mates, so a male falcon delivering food may be afraid to land near a hungry female, even if she is his partner. Instead, he may drop the food in midair for her to catch. Or he may pass it to her, foot-to-foot, as she swoops upside down beneath him.

The female falcon's feet are dangerous weapons and the male must be careful not to be injured accidentally.

A pair of falcons will breed in an area only if there is a good place to nest. Even when the hunting is good, the birds will move somewhere else if they cannot find a safe nesting site.

Falcons never build their own nest. For example, merlins often use the old stick nest of a raven, crow, or magpie. Peregrines, gyrfalcons, and prairie falcons may also use the old nests of other birds, but more often they nest on a bare ledge, high on a cliff.

The small kestrel is the least able to defend itself and its young from enemies. For this reason, the kestrel usually hides its nest safely inside an old woodpecker hole, or in a crack in a cliff or hollow tree. Kestrels may even nest inside a box built for them by humans. A group of researchers in Idaho found that kestrels also nested in the wall cracks of abandoned farm buildings, in old chimneys, in hollowed-out fence posts, and even inside drainpipes.

Falcons
FUNFACT:

Kestrels have two dark spots on the back of their neck
that look like large eyes. Ornithologists think the eye spots fool
predators into thinking that the falcon is watching them.
This may discourage them from attacking.

When the American kestrel is perched, it often has the habit of bobbing its head. This movement makes its false eye spots even more convincing to a nearby predator.

After many years, a gyrfalcon nesting ledge gets stained with droppings. Orange jewel lichens (LIKE-enz) grow well in these droppings and biologists can often find hidden nests by looking for these patches of orange on the cliffs.

Falcons prefer cliff ledges that have a floor of loose dirt or fine gravel, and an overhang that protects them from hail and rain and shades them from the hot afternoon sun. In some areas, such ledges are rare, so when the falcons find one, they may use it for a long time.

Researchers in Alaska found a ledge that had been used by nesting peregrines for at least 100 years. A gyrfalcon nesting ledge discovered in Arctic Canada was used for so many years that it was buried under 2 feet (60 centimeters) of bones mixed with old falcon droppings. The bones belonged to Arctic hares eaten by the birds.

Ornithologists in England have discovered a ledge that peregrines have used for over 800 years. In Australia, falcons have used one ledge for at least 16,000 years! At the beginning of that time, there were no humans living in North America, and most of Canada was buried under ice 1 mile (1.6 kilometers) thick. In California, there were elephants and sabertooth tigers roaming the land.

Most birds of prey tend to avoid humans and nest away from cities and their skyscrapers. However, in the last 25 years, two species of falcons have settled into city life.

Some merlins that used to nest in the prairies of Canada and fly south every winter now live year-round in large prairie cities such as Calgary, Edmonton, Saskatoon, and Regina. These adaptable falcons live in the suburbs and nest in evergreen trees where there are old nests built by crows and magpies, and where there is a steady supply of house sparrows for food. One ornithologist called house sparrows "rats with wings" because there are so many of them living in our cities. It seems the merlins have discovered this and are taking advantage of it.

Falcons
FUNFACT:

Some falcons have been given nicknames. The American kestrel is called the sparrow hawk. Peregrine falcons are known as duck hawks. Merlins are pigeon hawks.

For six years, this female peregrine falcon nested on the same ledge on the 15th floor of an office building in Calgary, a city of nearly one million people.

Another urban dweller is the majestic peregrine, which now lives in many cities, including some of the largest, such as New York, Chicago, Milwaukee, and Seattle. Most of these big-city falcons nest on the ledges of high-rise buildings surrounded by traffic and crowds. They hunt pigeons, robins, and starlings, swerving and swooping between towers of glass and steel.

In some cities, these nesting falcons are observed by hidden video cameras wired to television monitors below. Without disturbing the birds, interested people can watch the peregrines as they raise their chicks.

All of the falcons in Canada and the United States lay three to five rusty, speckled eggs. Many people think that the reddish eggs of the peregrine are the most beautiful of any bird of prey.

Falcons never line their nests with twigs, leaves, or grass. If the nest is on a bare ledge, the birds simply scrape a shallow hollow in the dirt with their feet to cradle their eggs.

The falcons incubate their eggs for 28 to 35 days. The two largest falcons, the peregrine and the gyrfalcon, incubate the longest.

Female falcons do most of the incubating, although the males may help for one or two hours each day while their partners eat, stretch, and preen. Most male and female falcons have at least two small areas of bare skin on their bellies. These thick, soft patches of featherless skin are called brood patches. They keep the eggs warm. Soon after the eggs hatch, the feathers grow back and cover the skin.

Falcon chicks hatch within one or two days and grow at about the same speed so all the chicks are about the same size.

Both parents are not often at the nest together.
The male must be away hunting much of the time.

Many animals hunt falcon chicks. They are called predators (PRED-uh-torz). Great horned owls, golden eagles, goshawks, Cooper's hawks, red-tailed hawks, ravens, and crows all eat baby falcons.

In Florida, yellow rat snakes and corn snakes may climb into kestrel nests and eat the eggs and young. In Texas, researchers have even watched an army of fire ants swarm into a kestrel's nest and sting the young to death.

Foxes, coyotes, wolves, black bears, grizzlies, and wolverines also consume falcon eggs and chicks.

It is no surprise, then, that adult falcons defend their nest and young with courage and force. An angry peregrine parent will attack any predator that comes near, including a human. Many scientists have been struck and injured by a falcon when they went too close to the bird's nest.

Because peregrines defend their nests so fiercely, other birds sometimes nest close to them to get protection from predators. Researchers have found common eider ducks nesting just 36 yards (33 meters) from a peregrine nest, and Canada geese nesting as close as 8 feet (2.5 meters)!

Many ornithologists believe that the bony flaps inside the nostrils of the peregrine falcon help the bird to breathe easier when it is diving at very high speeds.

When young prairie falcons are about one month old, feathers begin to grow on their wings.

The larger the falcon species, the longer they need to mature. For example, merlin and kestrel chicks leave the nest when they are about four weeks of age. Young prairie falcons and peregrines leave when they are five to six weeks old, and young gyrfalcons leave at seven to eight weeks.

Birds that have left the nest are called fledglings (FLEJ-lings). At first, the fledglings stay close to the nest and close to each other. After a month or so they become brave enough to explore by themselves. They may fly as far away as one-half mile (6.8 kilometers).

Even after the chicks leave the nest, their parents continue to feed them for one or two months. It takes time and practice for fledglings to become skilled hunters. The meals from their parents help them while they are learning.

Play is an important way for young falcons to practice hunting and flying. They chase each other. They dive on birds much larger than themselves, such as geese and ravens, pretending to attack them. They also chase clumps of thistle down blowing in the wind and feathers floating by.

One researcher watched a young peregrine chase a butterfly, and another watched a fledgling prairie falcon play with a dried piece of cow dung. The bird carried the dung into the air, dropped it, then swooped down and caught it again before it hit the ground. The young prairie falcon eventually landed, tossed the dung around, and jumped on it as if it were a mouse.

Some adult peregrine falcons are white. They are from the northwestern coast of Hudson Bay in Canada.

Most young merlins migrate south from Alaska and Canada in August. They spend the winter in Mexico, Central America, or South America.

By the time most fledgling falcons are three months old they have left the nest and their parents. This is the beginning of the hardest year of their life.

Only one young falcon in four survives to be one year old. Many die from starvation, unable to hunt well enough to feed themselves. Others are killed by owls, hawks, eagles, or other falcons. Some die in crashes with automobiles, power lines, and fences.

Today, the falcons of the United States and Canada are doing quite well. It was a different story about 40 years ago. After World War II, farmers began to spray a chemical called DDT on their crops to kill insect pests.

No one knew at the time that DDT not only killed insects but also made birds sick if they ate the insects. Then, if falcons ate the sick birds, the chemicals also poisoned the falcons. Poisoned falcons could not lay normal eggs. The shells on their eggs were thin and would crack when the parents tried to incubate them. Falcons could no longer raise chicks and the birds started to disappear.

This poison affected peregrines and merlins the most, but the other falcons also suffered. In 1972, the use of DDT was banned in North America. A few years after that, peregrine and merlin numbers slowly began to increase again. Today, these magnificent birds of prey are almost as plentiful as they were earlier.

People learned a valuable lesson from the results of using DDT. It was a warning. If chemicals can poison falcons, they can poison humans as well. If we help care for the environment and keep it clean and free of chemicals, then we and the falcons may continue to live healthy lives.

A prairie falcon will sometimes follow a northern harrier hawk and steal its kill.
Or it may capture escaping birds that are frightened by the hawk.

Internet Sites

You can find out more interesting information about falcons and lots of other wildlife by visiting these Internet sites.

www.peregrinefund.org	The Peregrine Fund
www.peregrine-foundation.ca	Canadian Peregrine Foundation
www.n-a-f-a.org	North American Falconers Association
www.adoptabird.org/	Adopt-A-Bird
www.EnchantedLearning.com	Disney Online
www.ggro.org/idhelp.html	Golden Gate Raptor Observatory
www.pbs.org/wnet/nture/exbirds/warriors.html	PBS Online
www.raptor.cvm.umn.edu/	The Raptor Center at the University of Minnesota
http://endangered.fws.gov/kids/index.html	U.S. Fish and Wildlife Service
www.animal.discovery.com	Discovery Channel Online
www.audubon.org	Audubon Society
www.kidsgowild.com	Wildlife Conservaton Society
www.nwf.org/kids	National Wildlife Federation
www.tnc.org	The Nature Conservancy
www.worldwildlife.org	World Wildlife Fund